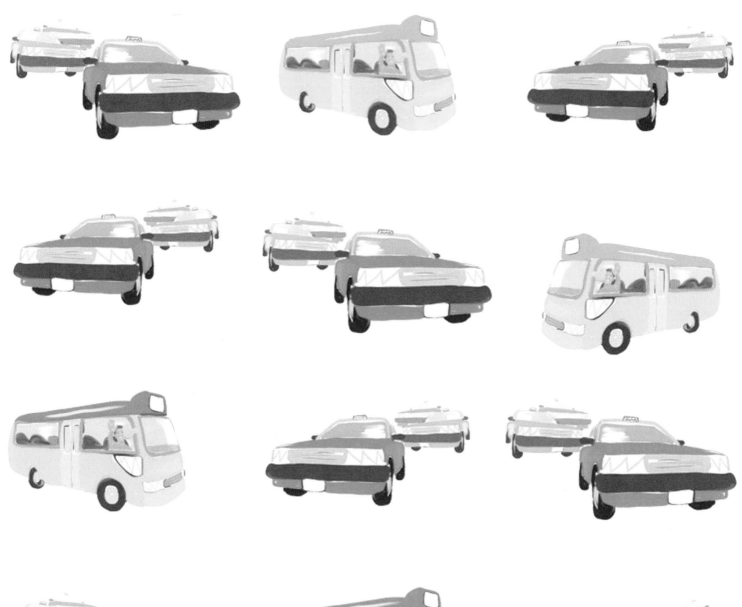

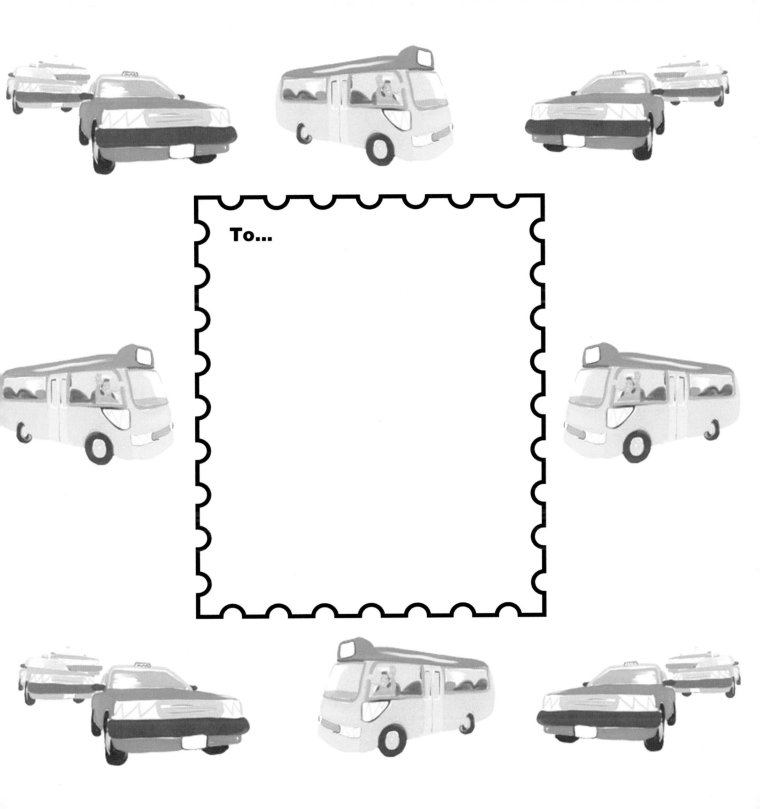

To...

I wake up each day
to a hum and a song,
and the sights and the sounds
that are my Hong Kong.

Hello bright red taxis
and green ones and blue.

Hello to you minibus
and a good day to you.

Hello towering buildings
that I have learned to call home.

And the hundreds of people
in each place I roam.

Hello there 'Star Ferry'
and the wonders you hold.

And the beautiful temples
with stories so old.

Hello yummy dim sum
and all your delights.

Hello smell of incense
that drifts to great heights.

Hello to the 'Tai Chi'
each morning in parks.

And hello stunning views
that have earned you
top marks.

Hello to the lights
making streets shine
so bright.

Hello soft, red lanterns gently floating at night.

Hello to the 'laser show' dancing up high.

And the big, watchful Buddha,
who waves from the sky.

Hello to the walks, the hikes and the trails.

And the many 'MTR' rides
that serve without fail.

Hello fearless 'Lion'
at 'Chinese New Year',
with the banging of drums
pounding deep in my ear.

Hello to the islands,
a whole other face.
So tranquil and peaceful,
with a much slower pace.

Hello to you 'Disney'
and 'Ocean Park' thrills.

And the endless construction
and powerful drills.

Hello to the markets,
the traffic and crowds.

I love every moment,
the quiet and the loud.

I finish each day
with a hum and a song

from a day of excitement
in my Hong Kong.

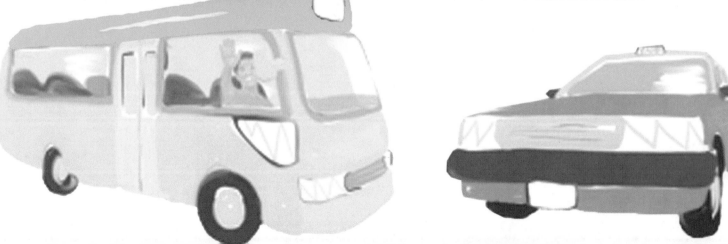

WWW.LOVE2READ2YOU.COM

CONTACT EMAIL: TANDT4STORIES@GMAIL.COM

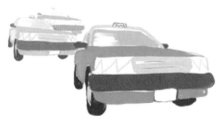

CHILDREN & FAMILY BOOKS BY MELISSA LAVI

MEET ELA-BELLE SERIES

KEEPING FIT WITH CAZ & KIT SERIES

SERIES OF OTHER TITLES

MY DADDIES & ME SERIES

Made in the USA
Las Vegas, NV
29 February 2024

86453677R00036